THE POWER DECK

THE POWER DECK

THE CARDS OF WISDOM

Lynn V. Andrews

CARD PAINTINGS BY ROB SCHOUTEN

HarperSanFrancisco
A Division of HarperCollins*Publishers*

THE POWER DECK: *The Cards of Wisdom.* Copyright © 1991 by Lynn Andrews Productions, Inc. Card paintings © by Rob Schouten. All rights reserved. Printed in Hong Kong. No part of this book may be used or reproduced in any manner whatsoever without written permission except in the case of brief quotations embodied in critical articles and reviews. For information address HarperCollins Publishers, 10 East 53rd Street, New York, NY 10022.

FIRST EDITION

Library of Congress Cataloging-in-Publication Data

Andrews, Lynn V.
    The power deck : the cards of wisdom / Lynn V. Andrews ; card
illustrations by Rob Schouten. — 1st ed.
        p.   cm.
    ISBN 0-06-250078-3 (alk. paper)
    1. Cards—Miscellanea. 2. Divination. 3. Self-actualization
(Psychology)—Miscellanea. I. Title.
BF1878.A437 1991
133.3'242—dc20   90–56474
                                                                CIP

91 92 93 94 95 HCP-HK 10 9 8 7 6 5 4 3 2 1

This edition is printed on acid-free paper that meets the American National Standards Institute Z39.48 Standard.

For Grandmother,
who taught me
the timelessness of truth,
and to Kathryn Duckworth,
for her tireless friendship
and belief in
the Power Deck.

CONTENTS

PREFACE

The Power Deck is the set of forty-five illustrated cards that accompanies this short book. Variations of this Power Deck have been used throughout history by teachers seeking to empower their apprentices with higher consciousness. The mystery schools, the Sisterhood of the Shields, magicians, and European shamans have used some secret form of the Power Deck for centuries. I understand from my teachers that cards are shifted and changed depending on one's time of life and the learning that is needed. These cards are for divining your truth and power in a way different from using a tarot deck. Using the Power Deck builds self-esteem, one of the most important components of power, by examining both the positive and the negative aspects of yourself, the pieces of your power and personal puzzle that are present and those that are missing.

I wrote about my first experience with these cards of wisdom in my book *The Woman of Wyrrd*. It was explained to me by the women in the Sisterhood of the

Shields that the cards were originally used to impart knowledge and teachings about the Tree of Life. The Tree of Life teaches about the evolution of the spirit. The cards illuminate the sacred flow and system of power in life. They help people to reach inside themselves to find their inner truth. The faces of the cards—the beautiful paintings—represent your physical body. The message on the other side of each card represents the truth of your spirit. Within the teachings of the Tree of Life, ultimately, body and spirit are one. The cards, like the Tree of Life, mediate between the life force of Mother Earth and that of all life forms.

I first encountered the Power Deck in my work with Grandmother in sixteenth-century England. (Please see my book *The Woman of Wyrrd* for a full description.) Catherine was my name at that time. Grandmother always stressed to me the importance of seeing that truth is always the same. Simply, truth is what is, and it remains the same throughout the ages, no matter in what time or place you live. What does matter, she told me, is that you become enlightened:

Grandmother reached into her pocket and withdrew a lovely carved box, which contained a deck of cards given to her many years ago by her teacher. Grandmother called it simply the Power Deck. "These cards are a way of finding the source of truth within oneself," she said. Grandmother then placed the box in front of me and nodded.

I opened the box slowly, as if I expected something to jump out at me. The inside was lined with red velvet. The cards were made from thinly pressed wood or leather. Inlaid on one side of the cards were beautiful pictures.

Grandmother instructed me to shuffle the cards gently while thinking of a question I would like answered. I was then to fan the cards out in front of me, picture side up, and hold my palms slightly above them. "Pick the card that calls you and read the answer to your question," Grandmother said. "But first, remember that in this teaching the cards represent your outer body and the message represents the truth of spirit. It is the same with the Tree of Life. The cards teach that ultimately your spirit and your body are one."

As I held my palm over the cards, I felt uncanny heat radiating from them. Then one card with beautiful gilt flowers on it caught my attention. I picked it up and turned it over. The message was "In death is the secret to life."

The message so directly answered my question that I was astonished. I told Grandmother that my question had been "What is the secret to a happy life?"

"See, the Power Deck never lies," Grandmother told me. She explained that each time we study and use the Power Deck, we create light like the sparks from a fire. "These sparks revitalize the life force that has been given to us by the land so that we may live. I must tell you that the source of all power is hidden in our mother, the land. To live we must partake of our mother's body. To engage in sacred study completes the circle. Studying or using the cards of wisdom, learning more of truth, gives off light. The beings of the earth live in a give and take, a flow of light, that becomes life force and then becomes love. It is law."

Exercising sacred wisdom in your everyday life literally creates the light that revitalizes the earth's life force. We owe a great debt to the earth and the animal kingdoms. Shamans and magicians have used the Power Deck throughout the ages to give to nature, to replenish the power it gives us. This life force is energy and becomes light and, finally, eternal love.

I send you joy and spirit on your path of heart and personal power.

Lynn V. Andrews

INTRODUCTION
TO THE
POWER DECK

INTRODUCTION

Please read this introduction completely before you begin.

If you could perform one act of power that would change your life forever, what would it be? Most of us do not know. We have lost touch with our own dreams, with that part of ourselves that helps us to manifest our true destiny in life. The Power Deck helps you to find that act of power that will change your life. By using the cards every day, you will strengthen your ability to find true harmony within yourself, and then you will manifest that harmony in the world. It is this harmony that will heal our great Mother Earth.

The Power Deck is simple and concise, but it is full of ancient wisdom that will bring you back to your true center, that place of power within you that needs to be heard and expressed in your life. We often blame others for our lack of power, but no one can give us true power. We must take it. So many of us today have sold out our power in one way or another, by choosing relationships or jobs that mean much less than what we had dreamed of. Perhaps as a child you wanted to make a mark in life—to change the world, or to be a great actress or politician. But you sold your dream for a job that pays the bills, and you are doing much less than what you had hoped you would accomplish in your life. Or perhaps you did fulfill your dreams but sold out through your body by not taking care of yourself. Maybe you are so busy that you don't get the exercise you need, and you have let your body go. In either case— selling out your dreams or your physical reality—you have become much less than you know you could be.

The Power Deck helps you go to the source of your dis-ease. It helps you find the primal source of your pain, or limitation, so that it can be healed. Pick a card each morning and place it on your altar of empowerment. Remove the "altar" from the Power Deck package, and let it stand in some important place in your home or office, some place where the beautiful painting can be enjoyed. When you look at it, you will remember your card and its meaning, and you will stop for a moment to move into that silent place within you, that place where truth is born. Take a moment to relax and contemplate the words on the card and the images that go beyond words, that lead you to a more profound meaning. Remember that each card promotes beauty, health, strength, and wisdom in your life, enabling you to manifest harmony on our planet so that you can become more a part of the nature and the beauty that is around you.

HOW TO
USE THE POWER DECK

The Power Deck can be used as a game of life or as a way to pray or meditate on your inner truth and power. Remember that the deck was originally an ancient oracle, designed to inspire you and support the power that is within you but perhaps has not yet been given life. The deck contains forty-five cards, forty-four of which represent the number of women in the Sisterhood of the Shields. The forty-fifth card is your Self card and represents the essence of you.

To use the Power Deck as a game, spread the cards in front of you, fanning them out or scrambling them with your hands, always with the picture side up and your eyes closed. Then pick up the cards again and hold them. Focus your thought on a question or an aspect of your life that you need to have clarified. Follow your breath in and out until you feel yourself settling into your inner place of power, your shaman center, an inch or so below your navel. This is your point of balance and equilibrium, the place where power lives in your body. Visualize your strength and power radiating out from this position. Lay down the cards and rub your hands together until they tingle, blow your breath of spirit over your palms, and begin.

Shuffle the cards, keeping your eyes closed. When you are ready, fan them out in front of you on the table. Rub your palms together again and then hold them an inch or so above the cards, scanning for one that calls you, one that is warm. Pick that card if you want a card for the day or to begin to construct your Sacred Self Wheel.

THE SACRED SELF WHEEL

In playing the game of the Power Deck, you will pull six cards to place around your Sacred Self Wheel—a card for each of the four directions, a Self card, and a Task card. Traditionally, the four directions represent different aspects of one's self or one's growth in the process of enlightenment. The first card you choose is for the south, which represents trust and innocence. It is the place of the inner child and the position of your physical being. When you pick a card for the south, think about that place within you that is filled with trust and innocence, where your inner child lives. Also think about how your physical body and accomplishments relate to the message. After you have pulled that card, place it picture side up at the bottom—in the south—of your Sacred Self

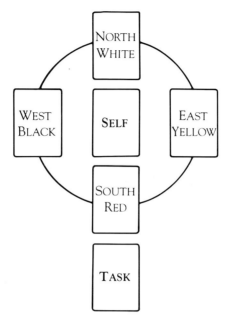

The Sacred Wheel

Wheel, which could be simply an imaginary circle in front of you on a table.

Now close your eyes and scramble the cards again, thinking about the direction of the west. The west symbolizes the sacred dream, death and rebirth, transformation. It is the place within you where your adolescent self lives and where your emotions live. When picking a card for the west, think about transformation from one life experience to another and how you felt about it. Think about your process of evolving. Think about the rites of passage of your adolescent child within. Moving sunwise around your wheel, place this card in the west.

Again close your eyes and scramble the cards. Rub your palms together until they feel hot; then hold them over the cards until you feel one that calls you. Pick a card for the north for strength and wisdom, for the place within you where your adult self lives. This is also the place of spirit and prayer. Place that card in the north on your wheel.

Once more, close your eyes and shuffle the cards. Then rub your palms together until they become hot and sensitized. Hold your palms over the cards and pick the one that calls you, this time for the position of the east, on the right-hand side of the Sacred Self Wheel. This is the place of illumination, of creativity, of the mind, the place of mental powers, often of wisdom. It is the place where the grandparent or old wise one within you lives. It is also the place of the sacred clown, the one within who tests your existing belief structures to see if they are valid.

Eyes closed again, scramble the cards, rub your palms together, and choose the card for the self. This is a wild card, because you can be as you are or become whoever you want to be. The Self card represents the essence of you, or the essence of your dilemma, within the center of the Sacred Self Wheel. It is the area that you likely need to work on the most to balance and mediate the powers of the other directions.

Now draw one last card, and ask yourself for another aspect of power that you need to work on—a task. Ask what aspect is missing on your path to power. Place this card below the south card. In the configuration of the cards, the upper cross—south, west, north, and east—forms the branches of the Tree of Life within the sacred wheel. The Self card represents the trunk of the tree, and the Task card symbolizes the roots of the tree seeking nourishment and wisdom from Mother Earth.

Before turning the cards over, look at the faces of Mother Earth that you have chosen. Meditate on the aspects of sacredness and beauty that the paintings represent and how they all fit together. To heal Mother Earth, you must first heal yourself.

Then, beginning with the south card and moving around the wheel, proceed to turn over the cards of the four directions. Meditate on the balance that is created by the messages on the cards, and consider what you need to work on most. Next, reveal the Self card. Contemplate the teaching, and see how it mediates among all the other positions on the wheel. When the information is secure in your mind and heart, turn over the Task card, which will tell you what you need to work on most at the moment.

Use the Sacred Self Wheel as a symbol for your personal expression in life. For instance, you may find in your soul searching that you live predominantly in one direction or another. You determine this by noting the color of the border on the message side of the cards:

South—Red

West—Black

North—White

East—Yellow

If you have many cards in one direction, you need to balance yourself with work in the opposite direction. If you have more than one card in the south, which represents physicality, you need to balance your physical activity with spirituality in the north. If you spend more time living in the west, in your emotions, strive to balance your emotions with rational work in the east, the direction that represents mind. It is important for you to bring mind and spirit into your physical and emotional life.

When you are finished, pick the one card of the six on your Sacred Self Wheel that you need to think about, and place it on your altar or take it with you for the day. Always gather the cards together carefully. Say a prayer of thanksgiving for the understanding that has been revealed to you, and put away your Power Deck. I keep my cards wrapped in red, natural material to protect them. Keeping a Power Deck journal is very helpful as you walk your path of heart. Over years of experience you will find that the teachings in the Power Deck will grow and deepen as you evolve and take your power in life.

AN EXERCISE IN
WORKING WITH FEAR

Fear probably inhibits some part of your inner expression of power. Therefore, your ability to manifest balance and harmony in your life is also limited. Manifesting your true destiny means that you have connected with your true integrity and power.

To help define your fear, try this exercise: Close your eyes and breathe deeply. Follow your breath in and out for a minute, remembering that breath is part of your life force. Take the Power Deck and begin to rearrange the cards, not looking at them. Be conscious of tightness in your stomach or some other area of your body where you feel uneasy. Rub your palms together until they tingle; then blow your breath across them. Now, fan out the cards on a flat surface and hold your palms about one inch above them. You will feel heat from the deck. With your left hand, choose the card that feels warmest. Meditate on the picture that you drew; then read the message on the other side. For example, the card might read, "Impeccability." Read the paragraph, thinking about what

13

fear might live within you that makes it difficult for you to be an impeccable warrior of power. Return your thoughts to the part of your body that felt tense or uneasy. Explore the aspect of fear that is hidden there, so you can then release the fear. The Power Deck will help you to experience your center of silence and power and help you to live there daily.

THE POWER DECK JOURNAL

It is very helpful to keep a journal as you work with the Power Deck. Each day's entry should answer the following:

1. My card for the day is . . .
2. The message made me realize my need to . . .
3. What I need to work on most is . . .
4. I am out of balance in the area of . . .
5. I need more clarity about . . .
6. My lesson of power today is . . .
7. My fear today is . . .

Now add any other notes that you feel are appropriate to your day's lesson. Over time, these journal entries will help you see your patterns more clearly, which will enable you to work on the areas of greatest difficulty.

A PRAYER FOR
DAILY EMPOWERMENT

A Daily Affirmation for Your Path of Power

I am a new warrior of spirit.
I exist in a world of sacred balance.
I balance with one foot in the physical world
of material substance,
and one foot in the dimensions of spirit and sacred life.
My course is set by my ally—the winds of time.

Mother Earth gives me life force—
the life blood of my sacred body.
The plants give me nourishment and healing
as I ride the windhorse of my intent—
my sacred warrior's transport of buoyant joy—
into a new and unknown world of harmony.

I am truly a new warrior,
an androgynous spirit being of light.
My weapons are the shields of awareness,

17

the symbols of ancient truth and the sacred giveaway.
Like the angels that surround me,
few see me for who I really am.

I do commerce in the world.
I raise my family.
I live a life dedicated to freedom.
I immerse myself in the physical world,
so that one day I can give it up,
because I can give up only something that I truly have.

People learn from me through example,
because of the integrity of my own life and spirit.
I move into the world with confidence and wisdom.
I am always open and learning tools of knowledge,
and I share these tools with my sisters and my brothers.

I am a warrior of the light,
and I live the integrity of that truth with great care
and from a center within myself that is pure goodness—
the embodiment of the peaceful soul.

I walk with confidence
the path of heart and personal power. Ho!

THE POWER DECK

— THE SELF CARD —

— 1 —
UNKNOWN

Center Card of the Sacred Wheel

We are all pilgrims on the path to the unknown. We sit in awe and wonder at the architecture of power. Ripen the receptive void within you, like a womb accepting a seed. Open yourself to the unknowable, to what is unfamiliar to you, so that the energy of what you need in order to be whole can flow into you. When you think of yourself as an entity separate from power, you will obstruct the current, and power will defeat you. Identify the form of power you want—what you want to accomplish, build, create, or be—and become that, so that there is no separating you.

Definition of the Card

The painting is entitled *Behold the Dream*. The Self card represents the essence of who you are as a person. It is a wild card, because it can become anything that you wish it to be, just as the self can become anything that you can dream. Here the pilgrim on the journey toward knowledge is sitting in front of the great pyramids, meditating on higher consciousness. The pyramids come from an unknown source of power. Because this source is unknown, a great power is retained within the structure: power is born from the unknown. Wholeness is represented by the spheres. This is a symbol of the natural human looking out into the universe of power and the mystery of the unknown.

— THE SOUTH CARDS —

— 2 —

BALANCE

South—Red

The structure of your daily spiritual life must be built on a strong foundation in the physical world, like a pillar of selected shaman's stones balanced carefully one on another. Take care of your body through diet and exercise. Express your strength in acts of power, and bring greater awareness to the exchange of money. Protect and nourish your family, and express your integrity by bringing balance into society and nature. Then you will be prepared in the physical for higher spiritual learning. Your being is like a spirit lodge, the foundation of which is rooted in physical manifestation—strong against the storms along the trail to higher consciousness. To take power, make your spirit available. Take your power and bring your physical and spiritual natures into balance.

Definition of the Card

The painting is called *Shaman's Vision*. It is about balance, with the shaman standing in the center of his world, choreographing the energies of his universe. He is rooted in balance and harmony, with the sphere of the universe and higher knowledge coming into him. Behind him is his village, well cared for with integrity and harmony. The eagle of higher spirit, who takes the messages of humans to the Great Spirit, flies over him, and a herd of well-fed caribou grazes in peace in the meadow. The painting shows the universe in balance.

Whether you know it or not, you chose to come into this physical dimension to become enlightened and to learn its lessons. Many of us want to throw away these lessons. We do not want to understand the exchange of material things, because we consider that a nonspiritual pursuit, when in fact it is a great part of our spiritual lesson. We must learn in the physical dimension to give away to the physical world and bring spirit and harmony into daily commerce and everyday life. Bring awareness to your understanding of money and physical things. Bring the integrity of spirit into your business.

Balance is a south card, because it shows that you need to balance your endeavors in the physical world with spirit in the north. To take power in the world, you must be in perfect balance. Realize the divine nature in humans and all living things.

COMMITMENT

South — Red

You need commitment to focus on your target, take aim, pull back the bow, and then shoot your arrow, knowing you will hit the bull's-eye with every shot. To hit the bull's-eye requires total commitment of your spiritual and physical being. You need only the commitment to walk down the path through the gateway into your true destiny. It is a process of gathering. You gather your emotions, your mental strength, and your abilities as you would gather sheep. It can be a long process, but your commitment gives you endurance. It is the next step after defining your act of power. Materialize your dreams and begin to live them. Build that magnificent dream lodge within you with total commitment.

Definition of the Card

The painting is entitled *Threshold of the Heavens*. It symbolizes our commitment along the path of enlightenment from one space or level of consciousness to another. This painting shows a moon gateway looking into the garden of higher consciousness and the sphere of universal consciousness within.

— 4 —

OFFERING

South — Red

Every day of our lives we take from Mother Earth our energy for life. We forget the ancient tradition of the sacred give-away. Take a moment to sit in silence and count the magnificent things you have in this life, even if only the wondrousness of being given life. Reflect on the Great Mother, Mother Earth. Ask yourself: "What have I given back to her lately to heal her?" Then think of the higher vision of life and balance on this earth, and realize that the greatest gift you can give this earth and your fellow humans is your own enlightenment. In this way you tear away the veils of ignorance and present the magnificence of your being to everyone who experiences you. Everyone around you is lifted and inspired. This is your offering.

Definition of the Card

The painting is entitled *Oblation*. It depicts a thanksgiving tie placed on an elm tree. The wind takes the prayer to the Great Spirit. The sphere of totality stands in a place of nourishment, a fountain, that is given from Mother Earth. The truth of Mother Earth is reflected into the boundless space of eternal life.

Offering is in the south as a teaching of the physical giveaway to spirit.

— 5 —

QUICKENING

South — Red

You can never really teach a warrior with words about the unknown; you must use experience. But if you look into the eyes of a woman of power, you may catch up with her a little. She has years of truth ahead of you. Her eyes can quicken you like a river heading toward the rapids. Open yourself with love, not with understanding. You cannot love with your mind. Listen from your heart. If a camel is walking down a path and another camel passes him, the first camel will go faster to keep up. This is how power works. Don't learn everything with your mind. Quicken your spirit by letting go of attachments and move to a stronger vibration of power.

Definition of the Card

The painting is entitled *The Search Party*. It symbolizes the journey of discovery on camels through the sacred land of the south. The universe is represented by the mountains. The sandstone represents the ancient quality of sacredness. The sphere represents the universality of power. To find power and enlightenment, you must quicken your vibration to a higher level by letting go of negative thought patterns.

— 6 —
FLOW

South — Red

The flower of your being begins to bloom when you move with the flow of life. This is a process of letting go, of moving your consciousness out of your mind and into your body-mind, which is an inch or two below your navel. Feel your receptivity as you become still. Watch the river flow as if you were a mountain high above. Be serene, at ease, and totally within your power. Then let the waterfall of life work for you, as you become like a twig carried on the surface of the rushing water. Become one with the river, dissolving the sense of mind and living totally in your instinctual nature. Let go, and relax into the eternal flow.

Definition of the Card

The painting is entitled *Flower and Song*. Follow the river flow. As in life, it is easy to float downstream with the driftwood but very strenuous to paddle upstream against the current. Because this is a south card, it teaches you about your physical self, about letting go physically as well as mentally. To go into the flow of energy in the universe, move into the instinctual side of your nature. The universe of stars and planets at the bottom of the waterfall indicates the universe of your inner self, of the highest part of your inner being. It is through this life on earth, represented by the mountain and the waterfall, that you can move into the eternity of enlightenment and sacred flow.

— 7 —
TRUST

South — Red

In love there must be trust. Without trust, there is no love. Jealousy is an illness of the mind and heart. Trust lives in the lodge of your innocence. The *heyoka* is a warrior of the Native American tradition who goes into battle backward on his horse with a broken lance, knowing that the Great Spirit will protect him. It is this kind of trust that you need. The imbalanced aspects of patriarchal history reside like stone carvings within each of us. Welcome the new aspects of feminine power in your being even though they may seem foreign. Trust in the ways of power and the Great Spirit. Know that you are made of power, and live with trust in your heart.

Definition of the Card

The painting is entitled *Time Has Come*. Pictured are two Balinese women. They carry parasols or umbrellas that symbolize the welcoming of the deities. The Mayan carvings are the rain god and Quetzalcoatl welcoming the feminine consciousness of the planet Venus in the sky. This is a painting of welcome to the new aspects of feminine consciousness in the south by the ancient aspects of patriarchal consciousness. This history resides within each of us. To find a balance of trust within ourselves, we need to know about our own history. Examine what is instinctual within you, what is male and female, and trust that you will find the answers you need to bring you into power. This will also bring those around you into trust. If those around you do not trust you, they will eventually try to destroy your power.

— 8 —
NURTURING

South — Red

We are the only ones who can heal ourselves—sometimes
with assistance, sometimes without. Our energy or *chakra*
system corresponds to the energy flow from the earth. If
you listen and feel, the earth will heal you as you heal
her—with the nurturing force of timeless give and take.
Prayer enables you to take power out of the mind and
place it in the hands of the deities of the earth and sky.
Try to see through the mirage of social barriers that cloud
the eyes of women and men the world over. Nurture your
dreams. Act in your dreams as you want to act. Find the
guarded kivas and sacred places where you have hidden
your heart, and nurture your spirit.

Definition of the Card

The painting is entitled *Morning Star.* The chakra system
or the energy system within a human being is symbolized
by the flowers moving from the bottom of the painting to

39

the top. The hands show that there is life in the mountains and in all things. The lotus is a lotus of life with the universe beneath. The fairy playing the flute symbolizes the vibratory sound of the universe and its importance on the path toward enlightenment. The fairy is bringing up the sounds of the universe into the chakra system of the human.

Nurturing is in the south, because it entails the life-giving force of Mother Earth. This energy is being brought up into human beings to enable us to have a complete circle of creative life flow moving through us at all times.

— 9 —

INNOCENCE

South — Red

A boat can represent your voyage toward the islands of higher consciousness. That boat is made from your treasured innocence. We are all born wild and innocent, like a blue heron. To live in civilization, at a very young age we become like sheep trying to fit in with the crowd. To maintain your receptive innocence is to listen to your own inner voice. Know that the powers of the universe are within you.

Definition of the Card

The painting is entitled *Vision Quest*. We are all pilgrims journeying toward higher knowledge. The boats in this painting are the transports to the islands of the unconscious. They return and bring messages to your conscious mind. The heron symbolizes the innocence of our being, and the spheres represent its wholeness. Have the courage and the innocence to move toward the mountains and fly off to the higher consciousness that is waiting for you there.

Innocence is a south teaching, because it is like the child within you. Look out at the world with childlike innocence. Try not to doubt what you see and what you imagine to be real.

— 10 —
SKILL

South — Red

Expressing your highest nature through your work is sometimes easiest when work is not exactly as you wish it to be. There are hidden gifts within friction. Therein lies the secret way to a graceful life. You are not what you do. Your work is a higher mirror, providing a reflection from which to learn in your evolutionary process. Then work becomes a higher skill, and you begin to fine-tune not only your physical self but your spirit. A Zen garden expresses the essence of life and a highly perfected skill. Come to the inner truth that produces true skill.

Definition of the Card

The painting is entitled *All Is One*. Skill is a south card, because it has to do with your physicality in the world and tuning yourself to your highest degree of accomplishment. As in all things, there is a lower skill and a higher skill. The lower skill is the ability to do something without spirit, simply doing a job. The higher skill requires finesse. It requires the perfected balance of your totality, of physicality and spirit. Then true skill is born.

In this painting a monk, a shaman symbol of spiritual activity, is reflecting on a Zen garden, where the stones represent different aspects of life and endeavor. In the center is the sphere of higher knowledge, of self-understanding of the inner world, which leads you to the higher levels of accomplishment in the outer world of true skill.

— 11 —
TRUTH

South — Red

Are you living your truth? Your being is like a spirit lodge. Within this sacred place is your realization and the divine light of your creation. Live in your spirit lodge surrounded by peace and joy. Outside your lodge is the great wilderness where the rest of the world lives. That wilderness can become a battleground stained with the blood of ignorance and earthly pain. To have lasting power in the world, you must earn the trust of those around you. Most people live without a sacred place within, without a spirit lodge, and they do not know how to enter the spirit lodges of others. Live within your sacred truth.

Definition of the Card

The painting is entitled *Touchstones of Eternity*. It depicts a sacred place in which to stay in touch with the universality of mind and spirit. This is an ancient Celtic shrine built as a sanctuary and a place to divine one's inner truth. The sphere of the universe represents the universal mind as brought down to earth by the antennae of the giant stone monoliths to give balance to our earthly consciousness, to help us find the truth of our own being.

Truth brought to us through the stones is a south teaching.

— 12 —
VIRTUE

South — Red

Virtue is one of the passive qualities of power. When you pull back the bow, preparing to set the arrow and define your target, you use the strength, the will, and the focus that you have collected within that part of yourself called *virtue*. Virtue is where you find inner truth. It is a place of illumination, and as that radiance grows within you, it becomes integrity. Without virtue, there is no inner balance. Virtue comes from the unknown, quiet things that you do for the world and other people. With each act, your spirit shield becomes stronger and more beautiful with the symbols of your inner life. Like the deer, they are quiet symbols. Virtue marks your path on the other side. Like the one who walks last, the virtuous person is in a position of power. Power often comes quietly. Walk in beauty and virtue.

Definition of the Card

The painting is entitled *Call from the Beyond.* An altar of sacredness, a sanctuary, is created in any place in the wilderness where higher thought is gathered. The monarch butterfly symbolizes the transformation to higher consciousness. The Buddha symbolizes the shaman spirit in reflection and meditation. The deer in virtue and innocence are drawn cautiously toward the spirit being. The abalone shell symbolizes the aura of light around the sacred space and being. The deer spirits imply innocence, caution, and beauty in the walk toward your own virtue.

Virtue is a south teaching, because it requires an understanding of your physical desires.

— THE WEST CARDS —

— 13 —
FEMININE

West — Black

The world is bereft of feminine consciousness. To bring Mother Earth back into balance, we must bring back our awareness of her. Language is a barrier between us, but woman has always communed with woman in an unspoken language. Her roots are entwined with the essence of Mother Earth, for she too is feminine. Woman is the Keeper of the Planet and must not let her energy be rerooted by the male systems within woman or man. We are all in need of world harmony. Mother Earth has been misunderstood, but she is the universe. She is the womb for all that lives. Feminine consciousness is the energy that embodies the wisdom you need at this moment.

Definition of the Card

The painting is entitled *In the Garden of Eve*. It is in the direction of the west, through the transformation of an overbalance of male energies, that we will reinstate the harmony and balance on earth, with feminine consciousness in perfect balance on earth and in perfect balance with male consciousness. The painting represents the feminine spirit as exemplified by the trees of women, trees in a grove of sisterhood, of women in communication. This grove of female trees shows its connectedness and harmony with the universal consciousness within the earth below. The butterflies represent the chakra system of energy throughout the human being, which relates to universal energies that are born from sacred space and provide a growing evolution toward the light.

— 14 —
IMAGINATION

West — Black

Exploring the wilderness of your own soul through contemplation brings you to the altar of your imagination. To have a circle of imagination in your being, walk with the untamed, wild, instinctual side of your nature, all the time knowing its power, like a woman aware of her own pregnancy and yet moving through the round of daily tasks. You need not focus on the unborn life for its nature to continue to grow. Remember always that inspiration often comes after reflection, after the seed of creativity is planted. When you actually begin your creative work, the energy of the universe comes to you and imagination flows.

Definition of the Card

The painting is entitled *The Path*. In the painting there is a path through the forest, and beneath the path you see a cavelike opening, representing the gateway to the west, into the universal spirit or unconscious. The sky is filled with soft white clouds, which represent your dreams in life and the sacred dream of the Great Spirit within each of us. Know that what you imagine is real. In this pragmatic life, we forget the importance of imagination. Imagination and visualization can be at the root of your successful ceremony called life. Power is often created through the ability to use the imagination in a pragmatic way. This painting is about primal passion, the origins of our instinctual nature. Beneath our seemingly simple reality is a whole other world that can be reached only through our imagination.

— 15 —
TRANSFORMATION

West—Black

The power of your intent leads you around the sacred wheel of endeavor. Begin today with trust and innocence in the early hours. Imagine a quiet pond, and see the reflection of your true self. At noon take a moment to close your eyes and dream. Image the transformation that this day offers you. Seek the strength and wisdom, through your ability to love, to bring this transformation into action and into the words you speak. At night give thanks for the illumination you have found. Know that the form of your intent leads you to the power of transformation.

Definition of the Card

The painting is entitled *Transformation*. The pond represents the serenity of your unconscious mind and the rebirth of awareness in the west. The steps in the north of the painting lead to a sacred place of prayer and worship of the Great Spirit. Find a sacred sanctuary within the universe of your soul. The lotus blossoms represent your transformation beginning to bloom, and the doves of peace take the messages in your heart to the Great Spirit.

— 16 —
DREAM

One day you will remember the Great Dream, and the
way will become known to you. You entered into life
through the veil of the Dream, because your reason for
being here must be kept secret from you until you find
your way home. You don't know who you are, but one fine
day you will remember. It is like creation looking for
itself. You are in oneness with all life, though you are not
aware of it. You will awaken from the Dream. Let the
Great Mother rest within your spirit. She is the universe.
She is the womb of all life. She is the light that shines
from your eyes, illuminating your daily dreams. The possibilities you dream of will become your reality.

Definition of the Card

The painting is entitled *The Celestial Dream.* It represents
the feminine power of the earth; dreams from the unconscious flow out of the woman's head into daily reality. The

lotus and the butterfly symbolize transcendence into higher consciousness. The universe at the bottom of the waterfall represents the spheres of your spirit and the life of consciousness within your being and within your sacred dream. Have the courage to manifest your dreams in your life.

This is a card of the west, because dreaming, transformation, death, and rebirth are part of your west training. The flow of the waterfall represents the energy of your dreams as they flow through your life and transform you.

— 17 —

PERFECTION

West — Black

Dream your passion. Fly away. Go through the hoop of your innermost fears and desires. Meet them and conquer them. What pain from childhood have you not dealt with? Move into the wound of your most secret fears, and find the seeds of wisdom that are planted there. Face what upsets you the most; it is a great teacher. Give away whatever is holding you back—insecurities, ego, fear of failure or of not being loved, fear of being alone—and be reborn into a new state of perfection.

Definition of the Card

The painting is entitled *Joyful Rebirth*. An eagle feather tied to a branch is the eternal giveaway of humans, four-legged creatures, and winged ones on the planet earth. To find perfection, we must give away what is holding us to this earthly plane. We must give away our addictions, the blocks that keep us from perfection. To reach perfection, we must move into the universes that live within our own souls.

Introspection is a teaching of the west. We must find the universal consciousness, symbolized by the sphere in the sky, that resides within our own unconscious. Shamans call this process *moving into the wound of our deepest fears and finding the seeds of wisdom that are planted there.* Grow from this knowledge into a state of perfection.

— 18 —
MYSTERY

A shaman can teach you about power. A magician can train you to become strong in spirit and competent in your endeavors in life. But to describe how a miracle happens or how you come to be a powerful magician is to try to explain the mystery. You can talk around the secrets of power, but if you describe them directly you lose that power and you destroy the mystery. Welcome the mystery, and allow the miracle of existence to emerge from the darkness and transform you.

Definition of the Card

The painting is entitled *Emerging.* You emerge into the mysteries of power and magic through your own intent. Mystery is a west card because it deals with introspection, death, and transformation into a new life, a new vision, a new way of seeing reality. The universe is shown here within the cave of the unconscious mind. True consciousness comes through an emerging from the darkness of our untold selves into the light of balance and harmony between the conscious mind and the unconscious mystery.

— 19 —
GRIEF

West — Black

Grief deepens you. It allows you to explore the perimeters of your soul. Grief is the only gateway to certain levels of consciousness, and it is a hard taskmaster. Through grief you can explore every aspect of your dark side — anger, pain, abandonment, terror, loneliness; and these are aspects of the sacred wound that in our daily lives we usually try to ignore. Grief forces you to look at those parts of yourself that are not yet healed. If you can look at grief as a teaching, you will grow. The pain of grief is not the only teacher in this life, but if looked at properly, with awareness and an open heart, it is one of the greatest teachers of all. The seeds of wisdom and enlightenment are planted within the wounds of grief. What is lost can only come back to us again in higher ways.

Definition of the Card

The painting is entitled *First Noble Truth*. So much of life involves suffering and loss, but great strength is brought

63

to us through grief. You can choose to learn from the experience and remain soft and kind, or you can choose to become hardened and cynical. Do not miss the lessons you are here to discover even in grief. This weeping Buddha, this symbol of the shaman going deeply within himself, into the depths of his grief, holds grief in his hands before a picked rose. The rose sits upon a stone altar on a bed of seaweed at the shore. The tide has gone out, symbolizing the elimination of desire. Final transcendence is at hand. The rose is one of peace, in the understanding that sadness and grief are only one side of a double-edged sword. The other side is peace, joy, tranquility, and the understanding that we all are one.

This is a teaching of the west, because grief takes us into deep, reflective thought, delving into our unconscious life to find the strength to transcend. In every death there is rebirth and transformation. Do not be afraid to learn the lessons that are to be found in grief.

— 20 —
HARMONY

West — Black

Harmony lives in the lodge of balance and involves equilibrium between the physical and spiritual aspects of your life. For there to be harmony, there must be balance. Imagine yourself as the hub of a sacred wheel, standing in the center. This wheel must function every day of your life. If you imagine that the south is your physical self, the west your emotional self, the north your spiritual self, and the east your mental self, you see that you stand in an ancient wheel of truth. Consider whether you spend as much time in the physical (south) as you do in the spiritual (north). Are they balanced? Are they in harmony? Reflect on whether you spend more time in your emotions (west) than you do in your mind (east). Adjust your daily life by being aware of your actions and behavior patterns to incorporate equal effort in all the directions so that your wheel will function in perfect harmony.

Definition of the Card

The painting is entitled *Sunrises in Eternal Places*. The painting symbolizes you sitting in the sanctuary of your truth and harmony. Surrounding you are the snowy mountains of your higher consciousness. You are perfectly balanced between the planes of higher, universal consciousness and earthly consciousness, as symbolized by the globe.

Harmony is a west card, because you must always reflect to find truth, which is one of the greatest teachings of the west. You must always reflect on how balanced you are among all aspects of your nature.

— 21 —
ECSTASY

West — Black

Ecstasy is a buoyant state of joy. One of the finest ways to maintain a state of joyousness is to examine the dark side of your being, that instinctual nature that most human beings repress in civilized life. Within your instinctual nature are the seeds of ecstasy. We tend to live in our minds, in our emotions, occasionally in spirit, and almost never in our instinctual depths. We are born as wild as mountain lions but live most of our lives like sheep, forgetting and denying whole parts of ourselves. Sit on the earth with your back against a tree, and get in touch with your roots, which move deep into middle earth; this will restore your joyousness and balance. Each day, listen to your body-mind and your heart. What are they telling you about a given situation? Ecstasy is like a windhorse waiting to be ridden — the last wild ride before your passage into enlightenment. Take courage and live your passion in ecstasy.

Definition of the Card

The painting is entitled *Rapture.* In this painting ecstatic femininity is a symbol of rapture. It shows that these stones are really alive, that nature is alive. True ecstasy is reached when we understand that we are a part of every living thing, that the sphere of universal knowledge is within our own process. We have already found our way home; we are already enlightened. We just don't realize it.

Ecstasy is in the west, because we must not be afraid to move into the ecstatic emotions that are within us. Do not be afraid to live in ecstasy.

— 22 —
SILENCE

West — Black

Before making a decision of power, move into that place of silence and serenity deep within you. Sit anywhere. Close your eyes and follow your breath in and out. On the third inhalation, take the breath down into your belly and locate your place of power just below your navel. Visualize your place of power holding the golden sun, a disk of radiant brilliance within you. Observe the silence like a deer in a meadow. If you are in pain, use your consciousness to find where the pain lives within your body. Then move into that pain and beyond it until you find the sources of silence. In this silence lives your sacred witness, that which sees all and knows all and is all that you are. Power is born within the silence.

Definition of the Card

The painting is entitled *Magical Appearance*. Silence is so very unfamiliar, because we distract ourselves from it, feeling terrified by the simplicity and the stillness of our own being. Like a deer standing in a marshland in awe of a magical appearance of beauty, we stand in awe of the magic of life. Because we do not understand it, we are terrified of it and often try to destroy it.

Within your silence are the teachings of the west. Accept what you do not understand, and have the courage to explore the mysteries of life. Move into that silent place within you. Find the ecstasy that is your true nature. You are the silence.

— 23 —
INTUITION

West — Black

From the left side of your body comes your female energy, whether you are a man or a woman. Within this femaleness, this feminine consciousness, lives your intuition. Intuition is the intelligence of your body-mind. You feel what is true with your body-mind, rather than know what is true with your mind. Intuition does not have the clouds of accumulated knowledge to distort your vision. Intuition simply sees what is the truth. With intuition you can feel the source of your being without reasoning it away and being filled with doubt. Doubt destroys your intuition. Find your power always in balance between mind and intuition.

Definition of the Card

The painting is entitled *Sanctuary*. Intuition is a process found in introspection, which lives in the west as shown by the portal of entrance into other worlds deep beneath the earth. This painting symbolizes the hidden universe within. The innocence of the deer, the monk symbolizing our spiritual being, and the sphere of universal knowledge intimate that we all are one: as above, so below. Intuition is a receptive power that leads you to your understanding of Mother Earth. The gateway to healing her and bringing magic into your life is intuition.

— THE NORTH CARDS —

— 24 —
FORCE

North—White

Force lives in your will and comes from your intent. Life is a process of pulling back your bow, aiming your arrow, choosing a target, and shooting. The degree and quality of the force with which you choose your target and shoot determine your power and your success. Force is built through your integrity of purpose, your physical tuning, and your balance of spirit and mind. By naming your act of power, you create force. Follow your innermost passions in life. Empower your will and your strength of force by manifesting your secret dreams.

Definition of the Card

The painting is entitled *Windhorses*. Windhorses galloping across the beach of our deepest unconscious symbolize the importance of force on our path toward power and enlightenment. Force comes from your will, which lives in your shaman center and has the power and strength of wild horses at full gallop. The windhorse is an ancient symbol for the state of buoyant joy just before the apprentice enters the plane of enlightenment.

Force is a higher strength needed to endure the trials of consciousness and the tests of power in the north.

— 25 —

IMPECCABILITY

North—White

Move into that place of perfection within you, that place of truth, responsibility, competence, and intuition. Collect your discipline, like a Buddha meditating in a garden of snow. Impeccability is an area of strength that continues to flame within, maintaining your power and intent. This flame burns in your center always, indicating the level of your capabilities and your effectiveness in bringing events into being. Impeccability is tended by the attentions of your sacred witness—that person within you who observes the target. Gather your power with impeccability. With the intensity of a rubber band pulled and held at its breaking point, gather your intent and focus on your impeccability, for the job about to be done.

Definition of the Card

The painting is entitled *The Bright Dance*. This is a painting of a snow Buddha, showing the centered shaman spirit within the stillness of a winter garden. The birds signify the innocence of the sacred spiral within life, and the stones represent the wisdom and the ancient memory of all life that is retained within the earth. Impeccability implies male action in the world, but before there can be movement outward as an explosion into the world, there has to be the impeccable feminine receptivity and stillness within one's being. Then there is true power and intuition within the warrior.

Impeccability is in the north. Hibernation and winter imply a time of gathering and going within, a time of letting go of what you do not need, so that you can be unhampered as an impeccable warrior of spirit.

— 26 —
GATHERING

North—White

This life is like the fulcrum on a scale of balance. Your past and future lives determine the need for gathering strength in this life. There is a reason for all the pain. As you gather knowledge from the infinite sea of consciousness and life experience, you begin to evolve. You fill the gourd of your spirit with knowledge, so that one day it can be emptied and you may begin to gather wisdom. Become one with all life, and consider the true importance of what you are gathering.

Definition of the Card

The painting is entitled *Gathering*. Gathering is a north card and expresses your need to gather knowledge from the universe, from the waters of your subconscious, so that one day in your process of evolving you may empty yourself of knowledge and begin to live in true wisdom. The native person in this painting represents your primal instinct and innate knowledge. The universe represents the *akashic* record, the totality of knowledge within all life. The stones represent memory and the knowledge of Mother Earth. You must partake of all to reach that still point of wisdom within.

— 27 —
STRENGTH

North—White

The person who upsets you most in your life is one of your best teachers. If that person can get inside your head, turn you around, and confuse you, you know that you still don't understand what you are doing. You need more strength. Learn by seeing that your life is a teaching. Like the red lotus healing its pain in inner solitude, gain strength from entering your wounds, and learn from them. The magician remembers the trail and takes a different one, even if it is more difficult. In this way, you build strength.

Definition of the Card

The painting is entitled *Unfold in Light*. It depicts a dense forest and a sacred being, a Buddha, healing his pain within the solitude of inner and outer wilderness. The red lotus represents the pain in the world being healed through transformation from the material into the higher realms of consciousness. Inner strength is found through deep inner search and meditation, particularly in times of transition. In the shaman tradition we move into the pain that we experience in life to find the possibilities for learning and growth that are hidden there. When you experience your pain in all its aspects, you can then move through it and emerge on the other side a much more powerful and strengthened person.

This is a north card, dealing with strength, wisdom, and spirit. By balancing your physical life with your spiritual life, you will find the strength necessary to evolve.

— 28 —

CENTERING

North—White

Never leave your center. Count your bad points as well as your good. What is good and what is bad are most often purely relative. If you sense a weakness within yourself, explore it. It may become the source of your greatest strength. As you sit like a sacred Buddha amid the pandemonium of your life, always remember that the situation or person who has the ability to upset you the most, to pull you off center, is your greatest teacher in the process of centering. Such negativity can become your addiction. Center yourself in your power, and release your need for constant distraction from your center.

Definition of the Card

The painting is entitled *The American Buddha*. Centering is one of the most important aspects of your training on your path to power. If you do not live in your center, you live on the perimeter of power, never inside the world of power. The Buddha image recurs quite often in these cards. To the shaman the Buddha signifies the higher self, the self that has grown out of worldly distractions. The fact that the Buddha is sitting in meditation in the center of a busy city implies that you ascend to the world of spirit and the higher self through centering, meditating, and focusing on the inner world. There is a city of activity around each of us, and around this Buddha there is much assault on the senses. By focusing on your inner self and staying centered, you can transcend the daily distractions and not be attached to them. Simply witness them as they whirl around you.

Centering is a north card, because it takes strength and wisdom to stay centered through the various tests of power. Looking at your problems as tests of power will help you to understand the teachings of the north.

— 29 —
ENDURING

North—White

Take a stone in your hand and meditate on it, or use the stone surface pictured on the card. Go into the stone. Experience her quiet soul. The stone welcomes your visit. Let her experience the inside of your heart. See how you are each an enduring mirror for the other. You are everywhere, mirroring everything. The stone absorbs you, and you absorb the stone. How can you be alone if you are part of everything? You are the totality of enduring existence. Therefore, nothing in existence can upset you.

Definition of the Card

The painting is entitled *Ancient Memories*. The stones represent the material world, and the flowers represent your inner soul and spirit. The salamander represents transformation into higher being, through the vortex of energy created by the sacred spirals of life. Stones teach us patience and enduring courage. Stones are the great storytellers. They were here before any of us, and they know the laws of the land. They are the teachers of silence. If you can become like a stone, you will experience the stillness of the stones, and then the flower of your spirit will brighten into full bloom with patience and enduring grace.

Enduring is a north card, because it teaches strength and wisdom in the process of patience. It is with patience and endurance that we understand time and the uses of power. Without endurance and patience your timing is never correct and your power is lost.

— 30 —
COURAGE

North—White

Action takes courage. We often feel like fish out of water, separate and different from the world around us. Fish out of water can learn to swim in a new air of consciousness with a new purpose in life. Perhaps it is identification with objects and clinging to addictions that keeps you feeling separate and keeps you from finding the source of your power: not only dependence on drugs, sex, or alcohol but also addictions like fear of failure, the need for approval, or fear of desertion. Discover your own power and meaning by having the courage to give up your addictions. Then live your power with courage.

Definition of the Card

The painting is entitled *Where Heart and Spirit Travel*. It portrays an idea beyond what we usually experience. The two fish swimming out of water through a forest are symbols of the transcendent spirit. They could be your transcendent spirit moving down the path toward the high Himalayas in the distance, toward higher consciousness. It takes courage to walk this path, to go beyond the boundaries of your ideas and imagination. Do not be limited by your belief systems.

Courage is a teaching of the north and a teaching of spirit on the path to power.

— 31 —
INDIVIDUALITY

North—White

When the shield carrier reaches the top of the mountain, she never seeks approval, because approval is based on doubt. Your strength and wisdom are celebrated in your unique ability to view the experience of life with new vision. Power lies in individuality and the ability to see yourself through your own eyes and not through the eyes of another. To be in power, you must take your power and exist within your own individuality.

Definition of the Card

The painting is entitled *Meeting the Members of the Board.* People are so stuck in their ruts of everyday life that anyone with unusual ideas cannot be accepted. The Native American chieftain in full ceremonial dress is considered a freak in this civilized setting in which the men are speaking of architecture and building a city. What the board members don't understand is that the chieftain is a great individual in his own culture, and he might have the answers to survival that all of us need and so many of us are afraid to hear. We are afraid because the answers may come out of the unknown, out of something that is unfamiliar to us. Because it is unfamiliar, we do not understand it; therefore, we feel the need to destroy it. That is our tragedy. To be in power, you must first be an individual.

This is a north card because individuality takes strength and wisdom, the teachings of the north.

— 32 —
WISDOM

North—White

If you are always addicted to the process of becoming, there are storms on your horizon. This is because if suddenly there is nothing left to become, you are filled with terror; suddenly you are face to face with your own empty being. Find the sacred space, a sanctuary of pleasant stillness in your heart. To know that you are truly alone is the first step on the long journey to self-discovery on the path to power. The final step is to learn that you are linked with the universe, that you have already become part of everything and already live in all the lodges of the universe. This is wisdom.

Definition of the Card

The painting is entitled *The Quiet Garden*. It symbolizes the birth of the universe into a sacred space. The sacred space is represented by the pagoda in the snow-covered rocks. The mountains and snow symbolize the stillness of higher consciousness. The stones beneath them represent the wisdom of all ages. Wisdom is found in the balance between universal knowledge and the sanctuary of knowledge that is learned through our harmony and struggle on Mother Earth.

Wisdom is a teaching of the spirit in the north.

— 33 —
ASPIRATION

North—White

Aspiration stimulates power. It is your aim spiritually and
physically in the world and involves the totality of your
being. Without the balance between the physical and the
spiritual, aspiration is a hollow accomplishment. It is like
a spirit lodge at the dome of which are your ceremonies
and rituals. But the spirit lodge must have a strong foundation of capability, trust of those around you, and
responsibility. Aspiration is what builds the spirit lodge of
power. It is the architect of your accomplishments and
sits at the feet of power, as the deer stands before the rem-
nants of an ancient and powerful civilization. Keep your
heart open, kind, and loving, so that the energy of the
universe can move freely through you. It is difficult to
aspire without judgment, but judgment limits you and
puts a fence around your consciousness. Give much con-
sideration to all your choices in life and a free flow to your
process of aspiration.

Definition of the Card

The painting is entitled *Eternity's Breath*. It symbolizes a moment in time. The deer in his innocence, in his quiet aspirations for life, is standing in the wilderness in front of an Olmec carving. The Olmec head symbolizes the ancient dreams of death and rebirth, past civilizations meeting with the immediacy of current life, the wildness of spirit, and the purity of nature. Aspirations revolve around the eternal struggle for strength and wisdom that are part of the north.

— 34 —
FOCUS

North—White

Much of what you see in life is an agreement that something is in fact true. To develop power, focus on one aspect of your life. This could be your career, a sport, or some endeavor that you have a passion about. Become an expert. In the process of becoming an expert, you fine-tune your whole being. You collect the important parts of yourself, and you begin to live the life of a warrior. Rid yourself of attitudes that are not essential to your task. Collect your energy and focus your power on wondrous and magical acts: let the shell of your consciousness rise out of the ocean of your subconscious mind. It's just a matter of focus.

Definition of the Card

The painting is entitled *Silent Sound*. The magnificent shell coming up out of the depths of the ocean, or the unconscious, symbolizes the spiraling primordial power rising out of the depths of our consciousness and into the reality of the conscious mind. The snowy mountains represent higher consciousness on the horizon, and the sphere in the sky represents universal knowledge. In order to have true focus in your life, you need to have balance between the conscious and the unconscious minds. For focus to endure, you need strength and wisdom, which are north teachings.

– THE EAST CARDS –

— 35 —

TIME

East—Yellow

What is time that it has such power to change all that
exists back into dust? What is this unseen force like the
wind that can shape the land and our lives? Learn to play
with time. Time is surreal, like fish swimming in treetops.
A person of power knows how to arrange time. Put on
your watch and be aware of the time at which you do
everything. Watch the sun, the moon, the transit of the
stars. Find out the time that Venus is lowest in the sky
before dawn. Be aware of your cycles—when you get hun-
gry, when you sleep. Our society is obsessed with time, so
now "become" time. If you're obsessed with something, it
is better to explore it than to deny it. Then it is possible
to give up your obsession and let a concept like time take
its proper place in your life. Your power depends on your
use of time.

Definition of the Card

The painting is entitled *Journey's End.* The symbolism of the fish in the treetops indicates the importance of the Tree of Life and the knowledge therein that we are, indeed, all one.

This is a teaching of the east. The Piscean era is symbolized by the fish, and it means that we are coming to the end of a period and are giving birth to a new aeon. Within this new birth, all possibility is at hand. Take your power now and try to understand what time really means to you on your path of heart. Do not waste your time; you only have a moment in this lifetime. On the other hand, you must have patience in order to create perfect timing.

— 36 —
MAGIC

East—Yellow

If you do not believe in magic, your life will not be magical. Magic, like the power of Stonehenge, is part of the unknowable—that which you cannot describe, but which exists and makes your life extraordinary. It is part of the goodness of your spirit. It is that mysterious and intriguing part of your spiritual life. Magic is what we are all looking for, but if you try to hold it and name it and describe it, you will lose it. You must talk around magic, describe what led you there, and give thanks for that part of the universe that is unknowable and full of color and strength and magic. Out of relationship comes magic. Out of the friction of forgetting and remembering comes magic. Out of the mists of dawn and the mysteries of creation comes the magic that we call life. Out of your passion for existence comes magic.

Definition of the Card

The painting is entitled *Ancient Astronomers*. To have power in life, you must take power. Power is never just given to you. Stonehenge is an ancient sanctuary and sacred circle of monoliths. The monoliths were carefully assembled to draw up the power of the universe that is within the earth, as symbolized by the spheres in the explosion of eternity beneath the circle. What is in the universe above you is in the earth below you.

To understand magic and illumination in the east, you must place yourself, standing in your power, as an antenna. Bring down the energy and power of the universe, and bring up the energy and power that resides within the earth. You stand as a mediator between the two sources of power. This is how magic begins in your life.

— 37 —

ILLUMINATION

East—Yellow

As darkness comes, the mirrors of your spirit reflect different images. It is the time when the world changes and your being begins to glow. Reflect on the new vision that has been living on the perimeter of your consciousness. An idea is stalking you and awaits your invitation, a place within you to begin life. The totality of your creativity comes after you have begun your work on the sacred painting of your life. It is then that the muses of inspiration surround you like eagles and cheer you on to illumination. Take responsibility for your work and your life, and then illumination will follow.

Definition of the Card

The painting is entitled *Liberation.* It portrays the liberation of the spirit. The glow around the body is the astral field of energy. The flowers symbolize enlightenment of the spirit encased within the magnificent vase that is the physical body. This painting depicts illumination in the earthly realm, with the sphere of the universe behind and around the entire form denoting higher consciousness. The eagle of the east is the messenger from the earthly spirit to the Great Spirit.

— 38 —
ESSENCE

East—Yellow

Life is like school. We move through it learning many things, cloaking ourselves in environmental knowledge. You are on the warrior's path toward enlightenment. You must one day peel away accumulated knowledge like layers of an onion and move back into the source of your power. When contemplating a Zen garden, you find that the source of your power is the essence of the Great Spirit. We come onto this earthwalk like a giant piece of smashed mirror, every one of us reflecting the light of our god. The experience of life is a process of piecing together these scrambled fragments into one great mandala, reflecting the one source of all being. Like the center of a cyclone, we sit at the one point of stillness, the pandemonium of life circulating madly around us. Choose equilibrium, not frenzy. Live life from your center. The essence of you and the essence of the primal moving force of the universe are one.

Definition of the Card

The painting is entitled *Silent Garden*. The stones in the Zen garden represent the memory of ancient life processes and experience and, therefore, stepping stones to our own personal essence. The sphere represents higher, or universal, consciousness. The Zen garden promotes the process of reflection upon the outer essences of all life and the inner essentials of our existence as human beings. If you do not understand your essence, you have no power. Do not try to develop force, intent, and abilities without first understanding the primal qualities and wisdom of your essence.

Essence is in the east, because the process of discovering your essence invokes illumination.

— 39 —
DESTINY

East—Yellow

Your act of power is the key to your destiny. Like a sacred flute player enticing your truth of spirit out into the light of day, own your power, because you are made of power. An act of power comes from a place of passion within your deepest being. It is an expression of your totality, of who you are in the world. To find your act of power is to live your dreams. What would you do if you could do anything? Discover what that is, and then do it. To find your power is to find your destiny.

Definition of the Card

The painting is entitled *The Source.* It is about the source of destiny, about the birthing from the spirit dimension into the phenomenal world, as symbolized by the stone and the petroglyph of the sacred *kokopelli*, the hunchbacked flute player. The flute player uses sacred sound to coax your spirit into physical manifestation. The lotus blossom symbolizes the birth into your spiritual nature, your true destiny.

This is an endeavor of the east, because destiny, when found, exemplifies your illumination.

— 40 —
CREATIVITY

East—Yellow

Your creativity is like a story; it needs a voice, a way to be heard in the world. Creativity has moved into your hut. Creativity is part of your future life. People think that creativity is like stories, that it is outside of them, like truth or power. But it inhabits you like your own life force, and it animates your being. Creativity is within the crystal palace of your mind. You are about to go on a long journey. It is called your life. You will learn to heal the evil forces of darkness. You are a warrior in the fight against ignorance. The dark sorcerers in life are created within each of us when we live a life of unexpressed creativity, when we live someone else's truth and not our own. Define your own creativity and live that creativity in the world.

Definition of the Card

The painting is entitled *Crystal Palace.* The pagoda is a symbol for the creative self. It is open to allow for the openness of mind. If the pagoda were your physical body, the crystal would symbolize your spine, the conduit for your energy. The crane is a guardian of happiness and longevity on your pathway to eternal creativity. The snowy mountains symbolize the higher state of consciousness required for true creativity.

Creativity is a teaching of the east, because it takes strength to delve into the deepest part of your spirit and then to manifest the truth that you find there.

— 41 —
VISION

East—Yellow

There are times when you will have less vision, and because of that dimness you will become unbalanced in your seeing; you will see everything—every stone, every machine, every tree—as dead rather than alive. As your vision grows, sit still within the city, and begin to develop and to see that stones and plants and even machines are alive. Even the dead trees have passed through the gateway in the west. Their spirit carries the Dreaming Shield. Begin to see the life within every object. Begin to see the sacredness in things, their energy, their colors, their luminous forms—their shadow beings. Then you will become strong. See power all around you; it is you. You have developed true vision.

Definition of the Card

The painting is entitled *City of Light*. It is about knowledge, about the juxtaposition of ancient and current symbols that live within us all. Here sits a Vajra Satva, a perfected being, representing the east direction with thunderbolts in both hands, symbolizing the power of God within each of us. This being stands tall in centeredness, as we all strive to do. Do not be distracted by the surrounding buildings of commerce, but rather stay centered in your vision of sacredness, and rise above the ordinary pain of life.

— 42 —
RELEASE

East—Yellow

Anytime you are possessed by an emotion that you cannot control, know that it does not belong to you. Someone is sending negative energy toward you. Imagine that the negative emotion is muddy water pouring down through your hands, legs, and feet and into the earth. Or take that emotion into your hands and release it like a hawk—let it fly away. We tend to hold on to fears and negative energy in an addictive way. Release your fears and let power come into you. Create a welcoming void within, through the power of release.

Definition of the Card

The painting is entitled *On Spirit Wings*. Release is one of the most important acts that you can learn on your path to power. Release lives in the east and in this painting is symbolized by the hawk flying toward freedom, with the sphere of universal knowledge behind him in a crevice of the mountains. The mountains symbolize the knowledge and wisdom of Mother Earth and the timelessness of memory that you can experience only after release.

— 43 —
MASCULINE

East—Yellow

Carrying your gift of consciousness from the heart of woman, of Mother Earth, trek toward the summit of higher knowledge. Because of male and female imbalances, the earth is in danger of dying. Remember that the power of the masculine explodes as the power of the feminine implodes, and a sacred spiral of life is set into motion. One cannot live without the other. The masculine God is in search of the feminine Goddess. He brings gifts of driving force to her powers of intuitive, creative receptivity. Both are equal warriors in the fight against ignorance. Balance your masculine and feminine energies through meditation and awareness of when you are carrying a male or female shield. This is your struggle in life and a great source of power for you.

Definition of the Card

The painting is entitled *The Ascent.* It depicts man, as a sacred being, carrying his gift of clarity and knowledge, which has been given him from the universal knowledge held within woman and Mother Earth. The stones represent the ancient memory of the earth. The mountains are the snow-covered peaks of higher wisdom. He is moving toward the sky and the sphere of universal knowledge.

Masculine energy lives in the east, because illumination for the masculine side of your nature is found through the mind, whether you are a man or a woman.

— 44 —
WITNESS

East—Yellow

Live in your sacred witness. That inner place of silence and observing is your true identity and therefore your true power. It is all you really have when all else is gone. Like monoliths in an ancient valley, the great stones observe and remember the passage of the ages. The answers that you find through the timelessness of spirituality and the innocence of nature offer the infinite. Each human being is on his or her own path, each different from yours. Answers to your questions are rarely found in another human. Answer your own questions by reflecting on nature and conversing with your own sacred witness.

Definition of the Card

The painting is entitled *Silent Watchman*. These monoliths are a testimony to time gone by, to the oceans of consciousness and unconsciousness that have existed before us. The stone monuments also represent the human in the passage of time and the universality of truth that is held within Mother Earth. It is important to learn to stand still, in silence, in the sacred witness within you. Meditate on stones and the great rock formations that have lived through the ages. Move into the essence of those stones. Through the stillness you become aware of, you will begin to experience the sacred witness that lives inside you.

This is a teaching of the east, because the sacred witness is, in the end, all that you have, but it takes great wisdom and illumination to become your sacred witness.

— 45 —
HUMOR

East—Yellow

Humor, fear, and anger awaken the power of your will. In the juxtaposition of realities, find truth, as in the primitive positioned in the wilderness of an urban setting. See how you have chosen your illusions, as others have, and seek to feel the laughter that holds together your daily dream. Self-importance blinds you to the source of joy and humor. Awaken the power of your will, and find your joy and your laughter. Awaken your sense of humor.

Definition of the Card

The painting is entitled *The Time Machine*. Life is often surreal, with aspects of the primitive juxtaposed against the realities of our current civilized life. We need our sense of humor to remember that it is dangerous to be caught in the dream, to lose the understanding that the reality of life as we know it is only an illusion. One day we will awaken and understand what we have really come here to do. If we lose ourselves in self-importance and ego, we also lose our sense of humor and our understanding of truth and reality.

This is an east card. It is part of your process toward illumination. It is a card of the mind, or in this case, perhaps, of losing the mind, setting the mind aside, and living in that state of humor that puts everything in perspective. Humor takes you back to your beginnings.

GLOSSARY

ACT OF POWER: An act of power is an act that you manifest in the world from your deepest passion. When you perform an act of power, you are manifesting your true destiny in life. You are living your dream.

ALTAR: In this book, an altar is a circle, a stone, an elevated platform, or any other focal point that is made into a sacred sanctuary by your prayers, meditation, and attention. Your altar could be a grove of trees, a corner of your room, a circle of stones in your backyard, or any other place you choose. The Power Deck package provides you with an altar of empowerment, an "easel" on which to put your card. Place this in a location where you will see it as you move through your day.

BUDDHA: The Buddha is the symbol of the Eastern religion called Buddhism, established by Guatama Buddha around 500 B.C. The many Buddhas pictured in the paintings represent both Buddhism and a sacred being, male or female, in a perfected state of illumination and silent prayer or meditation. The Buddha and other sacred figures symbolize the realization of inner truth.

GIVEAWAY: A giveaway is a sacred process of give and take. As a being of truth, you are aware of the life force that you take from the universe, and you give back that energy in like kind.

POWER: When I or the Sisterhood speak of power, we are not speaking of power over someone in terms of manipulation. The women of the Sisterhood are speaking of integrity of spirit, integrity of force, which is built within the spiritual warrior over years of practice, definition, and training. Power means that you have the ability and the competence to live your true destiny. Power implies that you are living your truth, not someone else's. Power means that you are seeing the world through your own eyes and are not living your life through someone else's idea of who you should be. You have learned to choreograph the mighty energies of the universe.

POWER DECK: The Power Deck is an ancient system for teaching an apprentice involved in any practice of higher consciousness about the truth, knowledge, and wisdom of life; it was originally based on the early teachings of the Tree of Life and ancient wisdom. It teaches through the understanding of the balance and harmony of nature and all life forms.

SACRED WITNESS: The sacred witness is that still point, that silence, that place of power within you that is not unlike the eye of the hurricane. Visualize life as a storm all around you, pandemonium, energy flows going in all directions, and you, standing in your place of power, in your sacred witness, at the center of all this activity. You need not be ruffled by negativity. You need not be swayed in one direction or another like a reed in the wind. You need only to live within your own place of power, in simplicity, in peace, always witnessing everything that is around you, taking it in but never holding it, letting it pass through you so that the next flow of energy can come. That is the meaning of the sacred witness. It is your shaman place of power, and physically it is located about an inch or so below your navel. It is your energy source and place of power.

SHAMAN: A shaman is a healer who may or may not be affiliated with a native tribe or culture. There are male and female shamans. Shamanism as explained in this Power Deck is a system of healing the mind and the heart through ancient teachings given to me by the Sisterhood of the Shields. These teachings have been expressed through many religions and in many ways throughout history, often with different symbolism and different icons, but nevertheless the source is always the same—the Great Spirit and the beautiful Mother Earth, who gives us life. The source of power is within us all and excludes no one.

SISTERHOOD OF THE SHIELDS: The Sisterhood of the Shields is a secret society of forty-four shaman women from around the world who are dedicated to the preservation of the spirit and Mother Earth through the evolution of wisdom. The Sisterhood has its roots deeply embedded in the nourishment of ancient times long forgotten. The women of the Sisterhood have protected truth as it was given to them, to be presented to the world when it was needed.

TREE OF LIFE: The Tree of Life is an ancient system for teaching immortality and the secret mysteries of higher consciousness.

TRUTH: No one owns the truth. Everyone has the right to know the truth and to experience wisdom in all its facets. But truth must be revealed carefully, because there is great power in the world and often people cannot handle that power until they are ready for it. Therefore, the Power Deck cards are designed to grow with you in their teachings. Each time you read them, the meanings will take on a different shade, a different texture, because you yourself will have grown and

124

changed. The Power Deck represents a universal system of truth on your way to power.

WARRIOR: In this text, a warrior is a male or female who is given to the task of tearing away the earthly veils of ignorance that surround us and destroy the perfection of our lives.

About the Artist of the Power Deck Cards

Rob Schouten was born in Rotterdam, The Netherlands, and received a degree from the School for Graphic Arts in Utrecht. His first explorations of visionary art in 1975 grew out of his interest in surrealism and symbolism. Schouten moved to the United States in 1979 and settled in Seattle, Washington. Since 1983 he has lived on Whidby Island in Washington's Puget Sound, an environment he finds highly inspirational and conducive to visionary painting. In 1988, Schouten and his wife Victory started Great Path Publishing. For more information about his work, you may contact him at Great Path, P. O. Box 882, Freeland, WA 98249.

Note from the Author

For the past ten years I have been describing my learning and my path. It has been a joy to do this. In continuing my journey, I would be grateful if you would share your insights with me.

Please write to me at the following address:

Lynn Andrews
2934½ Beverly Glen Circle
Box 378
Los Angeles, CA 90077
800-726-0082

Please send your name and address so I can share any new information with you about my work.